ANDREW JOHNSON

ENCYCLOPEDIA
of PRESIDENTS

Andrew Johnson

Seventeenth President of the United States

By Zachary Kent

*Consultant: Charles Abele, Ph.D,
Social Studies Instructor
Chicago Public School System*

CP CHILDRENS PRESS ®

CHICAGO

**Andrew Johnson
Monument in
Greenville,
Tennessee**

Library of Congress Cataloging-in-Publication Data

Kent, Zachary.
    Andrew Johnson / by Zachary Kent.
        p.   cm. — (Encyclopedia of presidents)
    Includes index.
    Summary: Follows the life and career of the statesman who
became the seventeenth president of the United States after the
assassination of Abraham Lincoln.
    ISBN 0-516-01363-7
    1. Johnson, Andrew, 1808-1875—Juvenile
literature. 2. Presidents—United States—Biography—
Juvenile literature. 3. Reconstruction—Juvenile
literature. [1. Johnson, Andrew, 1808-
1875. 2. Presidents.] I. Title. II. Series.
E667.K46   1989   88-39115
973.8'1'0924—dc19   CIP
[B]   AC

Picture Acknowledgments

AP/Wide World Photos—35, 38, 40, 49

The Bettmann Archive—11, 45 (top), 52, 57
(top), 83 (bottom)

Historical Pictures Service, Chicago—5, 6, 9, 18,
24, 26, 41, 43, 44, 47, 50, 51, 53 (2 pictures),
54, 57 (bottom), 58 (2 pictures), 60, 63, 65 (2
pictures), 67, 68, 72 (2 pictures), 73, 74, 76, 79
(3 pictures), 80, 89

Andrew Johnson National Historic Site—20, 42,
61, 87

Library of Congress—14, 75

Paul A. Moore, Tennessee Conservation
Department—4, 23

National Portrait Gallery, Smithsonian
Institution—28

North Wind Picture Archives—8, 13, 29, 36, 66,
83 (top)

Phortri—45 (bottom), 84

U.S. Bureau of Printing and Engraving—2

Cover design and illustration
by Steven Gaston Dobson

**Both sides of a medal
commemorating the inauguration
of Andrew Johnson as president**

Table of Contents

South Carolina secessionists unfurl the "states' rights flag."

Chapter 1

"I Am a Union Man!"

Northerners and southerners glared at one another across the Senate chamber. Once-friendly senators now scarcely bowed or showed each other the slightest respect. On some days fistfights erupted; angry men waved canes, shouted threats, and challenged enemies to duels. Senator James Hammond of South Carolina remarked, "Every Congressman is armed with a pistol or a bowie knife, some with both."

In December 1860, the United States tottered on the verge of civil war. For over forty years a raging argument over slavery had been tearing the country in two. In the North, railroads were being built and improved. Factories were going up and thousands of immigrants were entering the country to work in them. Steam locomotives roared along iron rails, carrying products from one industrialized city to another. Northerners had no use for slavery, and many people considered it to be cruel and immoral. In the South, however, cotton was the major crop. Black slaves toiled in plantation fields, picking the raw cotton and filling up their masters' heavy sacks. Southerners depended upon slavery for the success of their farming economy.

A southern woman and her slave visit the marketplace.

The problem reached its final crisis with the November 1860 election of Abraham Lincoln of Illinois as sixteenth president of the United States. Angry southerners feared that Lincoln intended to abolish slavery. Rather than submit, many fiery southern leaders demanded that their states secede, or break away, from the Union. By quitting the United States, these secessionists believed they could protect their states' rights and liberties. Most northerners, however, claimed such a move would be contrary to the U.S. Constitution.

A broadside announcing the secession of South Carolina from the Union in December 1860

During the tense month of December 1860, northern and southern politicians fiercely presented their views in Washington. Each day excited citizens packed the Senate galleries to listen to the speeches. On December 18 a hush fell over the chamber as Senator Andrew Johnson of Tennessee rose from his desk. Dressed in a neat black suit, the fifty-one-year-old senator held his large head high. His jaw sternly squared, he gazed about the room with piercing black eyes. Although Tennessee was a slave state, people wondered on which side Johnson would stand.

Johnson's voice loudly echoed through the room as he now addressed his fellow senators. "I am opposed to secession," he insisted. "If the doctrine of secession is to be carried out upon the mere whim of a state this government is at an end."

To southerners he thundered the question: "What then is the issue? It is this and only this, we are mad because Mr. Lincoln has been elected President and we have not got our man. If we had got our man we should not be for breaking up the Union, but as Mr. Lincoln was elected we are for breaking up the Union! I say, no, let us show ourselves men and men of courage. . . . Though I fought against Lincoln I love my country; I love the Constitution. . . . Senators, my blood, my existence, I would give to save this Union."

Stunned by Johnson's bold words, northerners jumped to their feet and cheered. Southerners, however, scowled and hissed at the Tennessean. News of Johnson's patriotic speech swept the country. The *New York Herald* exclaimed that it was "the talk of every circle in Washington and was uniformly condemned by southern men." Northerners called the Tennessean a hero. Letters and telegrams of praise poured into his office.

For their part, southerners called him a crude, uneducated man and, even worse, a traitor. They hung straw-filled dummies labeled "Andy Johnson" by the neck and burned them. They sent him ugly death threats. "If Johnson were a snake," grumbled one secessionist leader, "he would hide himself in the grass and bite the heels of the children of rich people."

An 1861 cartoon portraying the seceding states as galloping over a cliff

Among southern senators, Andrew Johnson stood almost alone. By February 23, 1861, the state governments of South Carolina, Mississippi, Florida, Alabama, Georgia, Louisiana, and Texas had quit the Union. Meeting in convention, southern delegates elected Jefferson Davis to be the first president of the new Confederate States of America. Completely loyal to the Union, Johnson declared of the leading Confederates, "I would have them arrested and tried for treason, and, if convicted, by the eternal God, they should suffer the penalty of the law at the hands of the executioner." Determined to keep Tennessee in the Union, Johnson left Washington for his home in Greeneville at the end of the Senate session.

The Tennessee senator's railroad trip through Virginia proved quite hazardous. There was no question that by this time Johnson was one of the most hated men in the South. When the train chugged to a stop in Liberty, Virginia, an armed mob rushed aboard the car where Johnson was sitting. "Are you Andy Johnson?" demanded one ruffian. "I am," revealed Johnson. "Then I am going to pull your nose," the man yelled, reaching forward. In an instant Johnson whipped out a pistol and forced his attackers out of the car. As the train rolled from the station Johnson shouted at the crowd, "I am a Union man!"

At Lynchburg, Virginia, he faced even greater danger. Another crowd charged aboard, grabbed him, and roughly dragged him from the car. Men swore at him, spit in his face, knocked him to the ground, and kicked him. Someone found a rope and tied a noose around Johnson's neck. The frenzied mob pulled him to a tree. They were about to lynch him when an old man spoke above the noise.

"His neighbors at Greeneville have made arrangements to hang their Senator on his arrival," he shouted. "Virginians have no right to deprive them of that privilege."

Only these mocking words saved Andrew Johnson's life. The jeering mob let him go to meet his fate in Tennessee. Arriving in his home state at last, Johnson bravely traveled from county to county speaking against secession. Often crowds hooted at him and shouted insults and threats. Still the senator pressed ahead. At one Knoxville gathering an observer remembered, "I had never seen him so cool, so determined, so eloquent, and so impressive in bearing. . . ."

The House of Representatives assembles in December 1860.

Johnson's pleas failed to keep his state in the Union. As the nation plunged into bloody civil war, Tennessee voted to join the Confederacy. Branded a traitor, Johnson fled for his life. In the North he labored hard in behalf of the Union. As a southern senator loyal to the Union, he bore the hatred of his fellow southerners with courage and defiance. For his lonely strength of purpose, President Lincoln praised Johnson as a man "to whom the country owes a debt of gratitude it can never repay."

Once a humble tailor, Andrew Johnson had forged a political career by honestly speaking his mind. The Union and the Constitution were the things he treasured most. Elected vice-president in 1864, Johnson became seventeenth U.S. president after the tragic assassination of Abraham Lincoln in 1865. As president, Johnson would encounter enemies in the North as hateful as those in the South. Even when faced with impeachment, however, he would never swerve from his high principles. He would never forget his duty to the nation, North and South alike.

Andrew Johnson's birthplace near Raleigh, North Carolina

Chapter 2

The Son of Poverty

Casso's Inn in the town of Raleigh, North Carolina, rang with laughter and holiday singing. People from miles around had come to enjoy a Christmas ball. Hotel servants ladled punch for guests and carried plates of delicious food from the kitchen. In the yard, stable boys held horses and listened to the cheerful celebration. On that night of December 29, 1808, Andrew Johnson was born in a crude wooden cottage that stood on the grounds of the inn.

Little Andy's father, Jacob Johnson, worked as a simple porter at Casso's Inn. He hefted luggage and swept the halls, earning a poor but honest living. To add to his meager income he took on other odd jobs as well. As sexton at a local church, Andy's father looked after the property. On Sundays he rang the only bell in town, which stood in the yard of Casso's Inn.

Although he was poor, Raleigh citizens respected Jacob Johnson, and in December 1811 he performed an act that made him a genuine hero. During a party at Hunter's Mill Pond, Colonel Tom Henderson, editor of the *Raleigh Star*, and another man tipped a boat and plunged into the pond. Without regard for his own safety, Jacob Johnson jumped into the icy water and dragged them both to shore.

Jacob Johnson had rescued the two men but, chilled to the bone, he had ruined his own health. Within a month he collapsed while ringing his bell, and soon afterwards he died. "No one laments his death more than the editor of this paper," sadly announced Colonel Henderson in the *Raleigh Star*, "for he owes his life to the boldness and humanity of Johnson." Just three years old at the time of the tragedy, Andy Johnson was left fatherless.

Polly McDonough Johnson did her best to care for her two sons, William and Andy. Working long hours spinning and weaving cloth, she earned just enough to put food on the table. Other families paid money to send their children to the local subscription school. In his entire life, however, poor Andy Johnson was never able to attend a single day of school. Instead he cheerfully helped his mother by chopping firewood and doing other chores. A spirited youth, Andy was considered the leader among his playmates when they went swimming or hunting in the woods.

Although Polly Johnson remarried in 1814, her second husband, Turner Dougherty, did not earn much money. The family continued to live very humbly. Years later Andy looked back and explained, "If being poor was a crime . . . I should have to plead that I was guilty." At last, in 1822, Polly Johnson apprenticed her sons to James J. Selby, the town tailor. By the terms of the agreement, thirteen-year-old Andy would work as an apprentice tailor in exchange for food and clothing until he reached adulthood.

Sitting on a workbench with needle and thread, young Andy learned the tailoring trade. Day in and day out he cut and sewed coats and trousers for men and boys. The foreman of the tailor shop, James Litchford, admired Andy's liveliness. He later described Andy as "a wild, harum-scarum boy with no unhonorable traits." Sometimes to entertain Andy and the other tailors while they worked, Litchford read aloud from newspapers and books. On other days a man named Dr. Hill visited the shop to read from a collection of the world's great political speeches. Fascinated by the stirring words he heard, Andy trained his own voice by speaking slowly and deliberately. Dr. Hill rewarded the boy's interest and enthusiasm by presenting him with the book and helping him with his ABCs. At home, late at night, Andy leafed through the book's pages and painstakingly taught himself to read. After that, he excitedly read every book he could find.

At the age of sixteen an incident occurred that changed Andy's life. Always full of zest, one night he and some other "bound boys" pulled a prank by rocking an old lady's little house back and forth on its foundation. When the angry woman threatened to have them arrested, Andy and his brother hurriedly left town.

In an attempt to capture the runaways who had broken their contract with him, James Selby published a notice in the *Raleigh Gazette* on June 24, 1824. "TEN DOLLARS REWARD," the bounty announcement offered. "Ran away from the Subscriber on the night of the 15th instant, two apprentice boys, legally bound, named William and Andrew Johnson. . . . I will pay the above Reward to any person who will deliver said apprentices to me in Raleigh, or I will give the above Reward for Andrew Johnson alone."

Ten Dollars Reward.

RAN AWAY from the Subscriber, on the night of the 15th instant, two apprentice boys, legally bound, named WILLIAM and AN DREW JOHNSON The former is of a dark complexion, black hair, eyes, and habits. They are much of a height, about 5 feet 4 or 5 inches The latter is very fleshy freckled face, light hair, and fair complexion. They went off with two other apprentices, advertised by Messrs Wm. & Chas. Fowler When they went away, they were well clad—blue cloth coats, light colored homespun coats, and new hats, the maker's name in the crown of the hats, is Theodore Clark. I will pay the above Reward to any person who will deliver said apprentices to me in Raleigh, or I will give the above Reward for Andrew Johnson alone

All persons are cautioned against harboring or employing said apprentices, on pain of being prosecuted.

JAMES J. SELBY, Tailor.

Raleigh, N. C. June 24, 1824   26 3t

The reward notice for the recapture of the runaways William and Andrew Johnson in 1824

The Johnson boys fled for several days before stopping in the town of Carthage, seventy-five miles away. In a rented shack Andy operated his own tailoring business for a few months. Then he moved farther south to Laurens, South Carolina, where he worked another year. In the spring of 1826, out of money and out of work, Andy finally returned to Raleigh. He apologized to Mr. Selby, but by that time the tailor bitterly refused to take him back. Still, the chance that he might be arrested hung over Andy's head. Neighbors had often spoken of Tennessee, across the Blue Ridge Mountains, as a land of opportunity. In August 1826, at the age of seventeen, Andy Johnson decided to travel west to seek a fresh start in life.

Andy helped load a two-wheeled wooden cart with all of the family's possessions. Along with his brother, mother, and stepfather he soon began his journey. An old horse pulled the creaking cart over dusty roads, across river fords, and up rocky mountain trails. At night the family cooked over open fires and slept under the stars. Finally, on a Saturday evening in September 1826, they reached the end of their long trek. Nestled in a fertile valley between the Blue Ridge Mountains and the Cumberland Mountains, the little town of Greeneville in eastern Tennessee seemed a good place to settle.

The family camped in a field for the night, and the next day Andy set out to find work. Trudging along the Greeneville streets, the young man passed a group of female students from local Rhea Academy. Andy Johnson's dark hair and strong features greatly attracted the interest of one of these girls. As he walked by, sixteen-year-old Eliza McCardle shyly whispered to a girlfriend, "There goes my beau."

Greeneville's local tailor hired Andy right away. For a time he also found tailoring work in the neighboring town of Rutledge. Through the fall and winter months he plied his trade, cutting cloth from bolts and stitching clothes together. Once he became acquainted with Eliza McCardle, it quickly became clear that he liked her, too. The daughter of a shoemaker who had died a few years earlier, the charming brown-haired girl lived with her widowed mother. Soon Andy Johnson made regular visits to the McCardle house. By the spring of 1827 their courtship had blossomed into deep romance. Andy was poor but hard-working, uneducated but hungry to learn. Eliza gladly accepted when he proposed marriage to her. On May 17, 1827, eighteen-year-old Andrew Johnson and seventeen-year-old Eliza McCardle exchanged loving vows.

Andrew Johnson's tailor shop in Greeneville, Tennessee

During the wedding ceremony Andy could not write his own name on the marriage certificate. But Johnson intended to better himself. In March 1827, after the Greeneville tailor retired, Johnson immediately opened his own tailoring business. The newlyweds lived in the back room of the little shop. During the day Andy sat cross-legged plying his needle while Eliza read aloud to him. At night she spent many hours teaching her husband to write and learn simple arithmetic. Together the young couple struggled and prospered. Martha and Charles, the first of the Johnsons' five children, were born in this simple Greeneville home.

As a tailor, Johnson became well known in Greeneville. Wealthy citizens hired him to make handsome suits. Andy preferred the friendly visits of his working-class neighbors, though. Farmers and laborers often stopped by to chat. While Johnson sewed, these men discussed local politics. Johnson agreed when they complained about the power of Greeneville's aristocratic slave owners. As a result of his boyhood interest in public speaking, he joined debate clubs at Greeneville College and nearby Tusculum College. His forceful speeches on local and national topics often impressed his listeners.

Soon many college students also visited his tailor shop to talk and exchange ideas. One student remembered:

"On approaching the village there stood on the hill by the highway a solitary little house, perhaps ten feet square. . . . It contained a bed, two or three stools and a tailor's platform. Here we delighted to stop, because one lived here whom we knew outside of school, and made us welcome; one who would amuse us by his social good nature, one who took more than ordinary interest in catering to our pleasure."

Simple Greeneville citizens grew to admire Johnson's forthright habits and ideals. In the spring of 1828 they urged the nineteen-year-old tailor to run for public office. With the help of his many friends Johnson won election as a village alderman. Greeneville's well-to-do slave owners frowned when the tailor took his seat on the town council. In spite of their disapproval, the young man always spoke his mind and looked out for the interests of the town's free common folk.

Grateful Greeneville voters reelected Johnson as an alderman the following year, and in 1830 his neighbors showed even higher confidence in him. At the age of twenty-one, Andrew Johnson took office as the mayor of Greeneville. For the next three years he held that office and strengthened his reputation as a Democrat.

During his years as a youthful local politician, Johnson's tailoring business grew. "I always made a close fit . . . and did good work," he later claimed. As his shop became more successful, he hired assistant tailors. In February 1831 Johnson spent some of his savings to buy a house on Water Street. "Without a home there can be no good citizen," he once stated; "with a home there can be no bad one." Happily the Johnsons moved their furniture into their new dwelling.

Soon afterwards he purchased a small building on Main Street. Into its comfortable downstairs shop he moved his bolts of cloth and sewing equipment. Proudly he nailed a sign over the door with the painted words, "A. Johnson, Tailor." The popular shop was known throughout the town, and in the Greeneville streets happy children often sang:

"If you want a brand-new coat
I'll tell you what to do:
Go down to Andrew Johnson's shop
And get a long tail blue.

If you want the girls to love you,
To love you good and true,
Go down to Andy's tailor shop
And get a long tail blue."

The Andrew Johnson home in Greeneville, Tennessee

Although he bought eight slaves to run his household and help at the shop, Johnson's politics remained fully democratic. Defying the aristocratic class, he strove to protect the rights of the common people. In 1835 he decided to run for the state legislature. To become better known in his district he gladly debated his Whig opponent, wealthy Major Matt Stephenson. Farmers and hardworking townspeople cheered when they learned that Johnson was just a plain laborer. They agreed with his stand on the public issues, and on election day he won the race.

The Tennessee state capitol in Nashville

Just twenty-seven years old, Johnson traveled to the Tennessee capital at Nashville. At the statehouse one witness soon took notice of the earnest young politician. "Though plainly clad and not so robust in figure as in later life," the man remembered, "his marked and expressive features presented him well and engaged attention when he rose to speak." Another observer recalled, "He was about five feet ten inches in height, with a sturdy, well-knit frame; he dressed always in sober black. His dark complexion and smooth face enhanced his great determination of appearance."

As a new member of the Tennessee House of Representatives, Johnson often voted against wasteful government spending. A country politician, he failed to understand the importance of modern transportation. When the Hiawassee Railroad applied for a state charter to lay tracks, Johnson opposed the measure. "A railroad!" he exclaimed. "Why, it would frighten horses." When he also opposed spending money for improving state roads, he lost his bid for reelection in 1837.

Growing wiser, Johnson changed his attitude about "internal improvements." In 1839 he regained a seat in the House. Whenever he addressed his fellow legislators or the common voters, his clear, melodic speaking style greatly affected his listeners. The citizens of his home district nominated him to the state senate in 1841. Johnson easily beat his opponent by two thousand votes.

As a state senator, Johnson soon enraged Tennessee's powerful slaveholders. For counting the population to fix government representation and taxes, the state constitution—like the U.S. Constitution—allowed each slave to count as three-fifths of a man. Clearly the law favored slaveholders and their districts. Citizens in eastern Tennessee possessed far fewer slaves than did residents in other parts of the state. In behalf of the easterners, Johnson angrily demanded that the three-fifths clause be stricken from Tennessee's constitution. Banding together, the senate's many slave owners defeated his proposal. Thereafter, many of Tennessee's wealthy class considered him their political enemy. Johnson, however, remained fearless. "Some day I will show the stuck-up aristocrats who is running the country," he exclaimed. "A cheap purse-proud set they are, not half as good as the man who earns his bread by the sweat of his brow."

Chapter 3

The Mechanic Statesman

Brown leaves crackled beneath his horse's hooves as Andrew Johnson trotted along the winding trail. In the fall of 1843 he was riding out of the mountains of Tennessee toward Washington, D.C. At the age of thirty-four, he had been elected to the U.S. House of Representatives. Reelected four times, Johnson would serve the next ten years in Congress.

Each day Congress was in session, Johnson walked from his simple boardinghouse to the marble halls of the Capitol. There he gazed about the great chamber and observed many interesting men. Ex-president John Quincy Adams proudly served as a Massachusetts representative and often sat reading letters and petitions from his neighbors. Congressman Abraham Lincoln of Illinois gathered men about him in order to trade jokes. Representing a Mississippi district, Jefferson Davis bowed with courtly manners upon entering the chamber. Johnson sometimes attracted attention, too. During a visit to the House, famous English author Charles Dickens saw Johnson's face with its dark features and penetrating eyes and called it "remarkable . . . indicating courage, watchfulness, and certainly strength of purpose."

Opposite page: Andrew Johnson
early in his political career

Henry Clay argues for his Great Compromise of 1850 in the Senate chamber.

As a congressman, Johnson voiced his opinions on all the issues considered by the government. Often he sided with his fellow southerners. He defended the institution of slavery as a necessary evil. Many southerners depended upon slave labor to support their agricultural economy. He voted to admit Texas as a slave state in 1845. Afterwards when war erupted along the Rio Grande, he also supported the Mexican War in 1846. When the slave problem threatened to divide the United States in 1850, Johnson favored Senator Henry Clay's "Great Compromise," which provided a temporary balance of power between slave states and free states in Congress.

A cartoon showing a new member of the Know-Nothings being sworn in

At other times Johnson sided with the North or showed himself to be fiercely independent. Southerners glared when he insisted that the Constitution and the nation were more important than the rights of the separate states. Many Americans felt threatened as thousands of poor Irish immigrants poured into the country in the 1840s. Soon the American, or Know-Nothing, political party sprang up to attack the Roman Catholic religion of the Irish. Repeatedly Johnson defended the rights of Irish Catholics. "Show me a Know-Nothing," he once exclaimed, "and I will show you a loathsome reptile, on whose neck every honest man should set his feet."

Always trying to help common people, Johnson fought for years to pass a homestead act. The United States owned thousands of square miles of land in the undeveloped western territories. Johnson proposed that these lands be cut into lots of 160 acres each and given free to genuine settlers. Hardworking people would build up the country while achieving their dreams of having homes. Unfortunately Johnson failed to get his law passed while in Congress.

Johnson still was concerned about his lack of education. In Washington he pored over books in the Library of Congress. He amassed many facts and figures to support the arguments he made in Congress. He developed his skills as an orator, and his rich, full voice often rang out during House debates. A *New York Times* reporter heard one of his stinging speeches and exclaimed that Johnson "cut and slashed right and left, tore big wounds and left behind something to fester and remember. . . . His phraseology may be uncouth, but he talks strong thoughts and carefully culled facts in quick succession. . . ."

During campaign seasons Johnson returned to Tenneessee and stumped across the state. The congressman's fame as a spellbinding speaker always attracted people from miles around. On foot, on horseback, and in rattling wagons they journeyed to listen to his voice. Johnson's words and beliefs reminded simple Tennesseans that he was one of them. In those days, people who worked with their hands—carpenters, cobblers, and other craftsmen— were generally called "mechanics." As a tailor, Johnson gladly took his place among these workingmen. When a debater once insulted his common background, Johnson shot back, "I do not forget that I am a mechanic. I am proud to own it. Neither do I forget that Adam was a tailor and sewed fig leaves." As Johnson's reputation grew throughout Tennessee he came to be known as the Mechanic Statesman.

Johnson's popularity and his independent political views greatly angered members of Tennessee's conservative Whig party. In 1852 these powerful Whigs at last found a way to prevent Johnson's reelection. They changed the boundaries of his congressional district so that it included many more Whig voters. "Fellow citizens," exclaimed Johnson to one Tennessee crowd, "the Whigs have cheated me out of Congress, they have torn the county of Greene from its sister counties, and attached it to a lot of foreign counties. They have split it up till it looks like a salamander. The fact is they have 'gerrymandered' me out of Congress." (The practice of "gerrymandering" got its name from Massachusetts governor Elbridge Gerry, whose supporters changed district boundaries.)

In revenge Johnson ran for the office of Tennessee governor the next year. Stumping across the state, he campaigned hard against the Whig candidate, Major Gustavus Henry. Famous for his speaking skills, Major Henry was known as the Eagle Orator. Even he, however, recognized Johnson's ability to excite crowds. "You have underestimated my opponent," Henry warned a supporter. "I have never met so powerful a speaker as Andrew Johnson." On election day Johnson triumphed at the polls and won the governor's chair.

On October 3, 1853, Johnson modestly walked from his Nashville hotel to the statehouse, where he took the oath of office. The forty-four-year-old Mechanic Statesman had become the Mechanic Governor.

The governor of the neighboring state of Kentucky was a "mechanic," too; he once had been a blacksmith. In a friendly gesture he tied on his blacksmith's apron, hammered out a shovel and tongs, and sent them to Johnson. Touched by these symbolic gifts, Johnson took up his shears and needles and sewed the Kentucky governor a suit of clothes.

As governor, Johnson set out to help Tennessee's common folk. "While millions are being appropriated to aid in the various works of internal improvement," he asked, "can there be nothing done for education?" At Johnson's insistence, Tenneessee established its first public school system. He also founded the state's public library, making books available to everyone. For the benefit of farmers and craftsmen, Johnson started regular state fairs. Each year Tennesseans could walk among the booths and examine livestock, farm produce, and new machinery.

Hoping to oust Johnson, Tennessee's Know-Nothing party put forth Meredith P. Gentry to run against him in 1855. During the campaign, Johnson and Gentry met and debated sixty times. Wealthy political enemies ridiculed Johnson's humble origins. They called him "low, despicable, and dirty."

In response Johnson proudly asked, "Whose hands built your Capitol? Whose toil, whose labor built your railroads and your ships? . . . I say let the mechanic and the laborer make our laws, rather than the idle and vicious aristocrat." A majority of Tennesseans agreed and elected Johnson to another two-year term.

As Johnson reached the end of his second term, Democrats throughout Tennessee proudly hailed him as their leader. The state legislature, controlled by Democrats, unanimously chose Johnson to fill a seat in the United States Senate. Deeply honored, the new Tennessee senator remarked, "I have reached the summit of my ambition."

Johnson journeyed to Washington, D.C., and took the oath of office at the Capitol on December 7, 1857. As a senator he voted against a number of projects he believed would waste government money. Instead he again fought to pass his homestead act.

"Like the air or like the heat," he claimed, "the public domain is the property of all, intended to be used and enjoyed by all."

The Homestead Act would not become law, however, until 1862 because southern senators from the slave states defeated his bill again and again. They believed that giving western land away to settlers would lead to the creation of more non-slave territories and states. Many northern senators wished to see slavery abolished altogether. As a result, northerners and southerners often yelled at one another across the Senate floor. Increasingly, southerners threatened to quit the Union and defy the Constitution to protect slavery in their states. As a senator from a slave state, but a loyal nationalist, Johnson found himself caught in the middle of the argument.

As the 1860 national election approached, four different candidates were nominated for president. The Republican party put forth Abraham Lincoln of Illinois. Many southerners worried that Lincoln wanted to end slavery. "What do you advise, Senator Johnson, if Lincoln is elected?" asked one nervous Tennessean. "As for myself," answered Johnson, "I shall stay inside the Union and there fight for southern rights. I advise all others to do the same."

Most southerners failed to listen to Johnson's wisdom. In November 1860, Abraham Lincoln won election as sixteenth U.S. president. As a result, within the next three months seven southern states voted to secede from the Union. Now, instead of fighting for southern rights, Johnson found himself fighting to save the Union itself. Taking the floor of the Senate, Johnson repeatedly insisted that saving the Union was more important than all else.

In one speech he patriotically proclaimed, "I say to every Senator . . . , to every man that loves his country . . . , if you are for preserving the Union in its great and fundamental principles, I am your ally. . . ." Of the senators from seceding states, only Johnson chose to stand by the Constitution. In March 1861 he expressed his anger at the latest actions of the South against the federal government. "Show me . . . who has fired upon our flag, has given instructions to take our forts and our custom houses, our arsenals and our dock-yards, and I will show you a traitor!" Thrilled by these bold words, northerners in the Senate chamber pounded their desks and clapped their hands.

The interior of Fort Sumter as it was being bombarded by Confederates

At the close of the Senate session in March 1861, Johnson hastened back to Tennessee. His journey home proved very dangerous. Southerners now despised him, and in Lynchburg, Virginia, a mob dragged Johnson from his train, beat him, and almost hanged him. Many Tennesseans greeted his return with sneers and hatred. Anonymous letters threatened him with death. In eastern Tennessee Johnson fearlessly rode from town to town, calling upon his countrymen to remain loyal to the Union.

In April the American Civil War erupted when rebel soldiers bombarded the Union garrison at Fort Sumter in the harbor of Charleston, South Carolina. In May, Arkansas, North Carolina, and Virginia also chose to secede from the Union and join the Confederate States. Soon Tennessee became the eleventh state to join the Confederacy. Calling secession "hell-born and hell-bent," Johnson fled north to save his life.

Chapter 4

Fighting for the Stars and Stripes

"We have commenced the battle of freedom . . . I say, let the battle go on—until the Stars and Stripes shall again be unfurled upon every cross-road, and from every house-top. . . ." Andrew Johnson's voice rang out in the U.S. Senate and his listeners applauded his loyal words. A senator without a state, Johnson welcomed war if it would bring Tennessee back into the Union.

Already in the summer and fall of 1861, many loyal eastern Tennesseans were fighting a guerrilla war against their Confederate neighbors in the Cumberland Mountains. In Greeneville, gray-clad Confederate troops took over many buildings. "My wife and children have been turned into the street," exclaimed Johnson in the Senate, "and my house has been turned into a barrack, and for what? Because I stand by the Constitution. . . . This is my offense. . . ."

The Union attack on Fort Donelson, Tennessee

In Washington Johnson urged the speedy recapture of Tennessee. Bent over maps of the region, Union generals soon plotted an invasion of the important border state. During the Civil War only Virginia would see harder fighting than the state of Tennessee. In February 1862 Union general Ulysses S. Grant struck a mighty blow. Cannon thundered and muskets blazed as Yankee troops captured Fort Henry and Fort Donelson in western Tennessee. Completely stunned, the Confederates abandoned that part of the state, including the capital at Nashville. To win Tennessee back into the Union, President Lincoln turned to Andrew Johnson. In March he appointed Johnson military governor of Tennessee, and ordered him "to provide . . . peace and security to the loyal inhabitants of that state until they shall be able to establish a civil government."

Resigning his Senate seat, Johnson pledged himself to undertake this difficult task. With the rank of brigadier general he hurried to Nashville to fill his new military office. With total authority, Johnson moved to rid Tennessee of Confederate influence. He fired government workers who refused to take an oath of allegiance to the Union. He arrested six Nashville ministers for preaching secession in their pulpits. He closed down Confederate newspapers, ordered railroad lines repaired and guarded, and also levied taxes.

As Shiloh, Stones River, and other bloody Tennessee battles claimed the lives of Union soldiers, Johnson toured western Tennessee and raised twenty-five fresh Yankee regiments. "Never shall we surrender the cause we are fighting for," Johnson exhorted one camp of new recruits. For two years the war swept back and forth across Tennessee. In the fall of 1862, Confederate raiders led by General Nathan Bedford Forrest surrounded Nashville. Within the besieged city Johnson vowed, "I am no military man, but anyone who talks of surrendering I will shoot." Several times the Confederates attacked and the Union defenders stiffly fought them off. "The coolness and calmness of the Governor amid these trying scenes are beyond all praise," exclaimed a *New York Herald* reporter. "He does all he can to preserve order." In the end, the Confederates retreated.

The Civil War battle of Chattanooga, Tennessee

Other Union victories followed, clearing the enemy from the state. As 1863 drew to a close Johnson gladly reported to his fellow loyal Tennesseans, "The rebel army is driven back. . . . Whenever you desire in good faith to restore civil authority, you can do so. . . ." With Lincoln's encouragement, Johnson worked hard to end military rule in Tennessee. Finally delegates at a state convention in 1864 designed a new state government and abolished slavery in Tennessee forever.

Not everyone was pleased with these changes. Confederate sympathizers bitterly resisted Johnson's efforts to establish peace. President Lincoln, however, praised the governor's great services and personal sacrifices. "No man has the right to judge Andrew Johnson in any respect," he declared, "who has not suffered as much and done as much as he for the Union's sake."

Pennnsylvania congressman Thaddeus Stevens

In 1864 Republicans and Democrats who supported Lincoln's war efforts gathered in Baltimore to nominate him for a second term as president. One delegate stopped at the White House on his way to the convention. "Whom do you desire put on the ticket with you as Vice-President?" the man asked Lincoln. Lincoln leaned forward and answered in a low, distinct tone, "Governor Johnson of Tennessee."

When Pennsylvania congressman Thaddeus Stevens learned of Lincoln's choice he complained, "Can't you find a candidate for Vice-President in the United States without going down to one of those damned rebel provinces to pick one up?" Vice-President Hannibal Hamlin of Maine had served Lincoln faithfully during his first term. Lincoln believed, though, that Johnson's history as a staunch Unionist from a border state would have broader appeal and improve his reelection chances.

The National Union party's campaign poster

On the first ballot Abraham Lincoln easily won renomination for president. In the vice-presidential balloting that followed, delegates picked Andrew Johnson, just as Lincoln wished. Together, Republican Lincoln and Democrat Johnson formed the National Union party ticket. "What will the aristocrats do with a rail-splitter for President and a tailor for Vice-president?" Johnson wondered with a smile when he learned of the convention's choice.

George B. McClellan ("Little Mac") having trouble in the 1864 presidential campaign

To Nashville citizens he soon sincerely announced, "I accept the nomination on principle, be the consequences what they may. I will do what I believe to be my duty."

The Democratic national convention met in Chicago in August 1864. It picked General George B. McClellan to run for president. Democrats claimed that the war was a failure, and McClellan pledged to end the war speedily by negotiating with the Confederate states. During the election campaign McClellan's supporters wailed about the war's continued bloodshed. The *New York World* mocked Lincoln and Johnson, calling them "two ignorant, boorish, third-rate backwoods lawyers."

An 1864 cartoon entitled "The Rail Splitter at Work Repairing the Union"

Unionists, however, rallied behind Lincoln and Johnson. One popular political cartoon showed Lincoln pulling a torn United States map closer together while Johnson stood by with needle and thread. "Take it quietly, Uncle Abe," Johnson was saying. "I will draw it closer than ever and the good old Union will be mended." In September 1864, Union troops commanded by General William T. Sherman captured the important southern city of Atlanta, Georgia. This timely Union victory, along with other military advances, showed that the North could win the war. On election day, November 8, 1864, a clear majority of Americans voted for the Lincoln-Johnson ticket. Lincoln had won, and Andrew Johnson would be the next vice-president of the United States.

Above: Sherman (leaning on cannon, right) and his staff in Atlanta
Below: The ruins of the Confederate capital of Richmond, Virginia

During the next few months Johnson hurried to finish his work forming a civilian government in Tennessee. On January 13, 1865, he finally wrote to President Lincoln, "All is now working well, and if Tennessee is now left alone [it] will soon resume all the functions of a state. . . ." Johnson's labors had broken down his health. Still he promised Lincoln he would attend the inauguration ceremonies in Washington that March.

An exhausting train ride carried Johnson, feeling ill and feverish, to Washington. March 4, 1865, inauguration day, dawned cold and wet. In the Senate chamber ladies in flowing satin gowns and men in pressed suits eagerly crowded close to watch Johnson sworn in as vice-president. While he waited for the ceremony to start, Johnson felt weak. He asked for a drink to help revive his spirits. Someone brought a flask of brandy and the weary Tennessean drank it down. As a result, when he took the oath of office he seemed dizzy and light-headed. Afterwards he turned and delivered a long, rambling speech. "Here even the humblest has a chance with the mightiest," he shouted. As he slurred his words, it appeared to everyone that the new vice-president was drunk.

The unfortunate incident caused people to shake their heads. Gossips described Johnson as "Andy the Sot," and the *New York World* wailed, "To think that one frail life stands between this insolent, clownish creature and the presidency! May God bless and spare Abraham Lincoln!" While others worried and complained, Lincoln was quick to forgive his vice-president. To Secretary of the Treasury Hugh McCulloch he remarked, "Oh, well, don't you

President Lincoln takes the oath of office on March 4, 1865.

bother about Andy Johnson's drinking. He made a bad slip the other day, but I have known Andy a great many years, and he ain't no drunkard."

During the next days the vice-president rested and regained his health. In April 1865 the Civil War drew to its bloody end. Four years of battle had greatly weakened the South. The destruction of its farms and factories marked its final doom. On April 2, Union troops at last captured the city of Richmond, Virginia. Two days later Vice-President Johnson walked with Lincoln on an inspection tour among the smoking ruins of the fallen Confederate capital.

47

On April 9 the North celebrated even better news. Surrounded by General Grant's army at Appomattox Court House, Virginia, General Robert E. Lee had surrendered his Confederate army. In Washington people wildly crowded into the streets to celebrate. Navy secretary Gideon Welles exclaimed, "The nation seems delirious with joy. Guns are firing, bells ringing, flags flying, men laughing, children cheering; all, all are jubilant."

The happiness lasted well into the next week. No one guessed that an actor named John Wilkes Booth had hatched a crazy scheme. Hoping that the defeated South could still carry on the war, Booth plotted the murders of President Lincoln, Vice-President Johnson, and Secretary of State William Seward. On April 14 Booth issued his final orders to his odd group of followers. A carriage maker, George Atzerodt, was to kill Andrew Johnson.

That same day, Atzerodt rented a room at the Kirkwood House hotel. The room was located almost directly above the suite where Johnson was staying. After hiding a knife and pistol under his mattress, Atzerodt stepped down to the hotel barroom, where he asked many questions about the vice-president's private habits.

That afternoon Johnson met with Lincoln at the White House. Together they talked about the future of the southern states now that the war was over. That evening Johnson invited ex-governor of Wisconsin Leonard Farwell into his hotel room for a pleasant chat. Farwell mentioned that he was about to leave for Ford's Theater. President Lincoln was expected to attend the performance of *Our American Cousin* that night, making it a gala occasion.

John Wilkes Booth

Not long after Farwell departed, Johnson prepared for bed. At the same time, his assassin aimlessly wandered the Washington streets. Having lost his nerve and gotten drunk, Atzerodt would fail to carry out his part of the murder conspiracy. At Ford's Theater, John Wilkes Booth madly stalked the president. At 10:00 P.M. Booth entered Lincoln's box and fired a pistol into the back of his skull. With eyes flashing, Booth jumped down to the stage, breaking his leg in the process. "Sic semper tyrannis!" he shouted, meaning in Latin "Thus always with tyrants," before escaping into the night. Stunned witnesses crowded the aisles. Screams and moans filled the hall. People rushed into the streets to spread the horrible news.

Secretary of State William Henry Seward

At the Kirkwood House a loud knocking awakened Johnson from his slumber. "Governor Johnson, if you are in this room, I must see you," shouted a voice. The vice-president answered the door and ex-governor Farwell hurried inside. "Someone," Farwell exclaimed, "has shot and murdered the President." Shocked and worried, the two men clung to each other a moment in disbelief. Then Farwell rang for servants. Men soon guarded the halls outside Johnson's door. Shocked people jammed the hotel lobby, and other panicked citizens crowded the street, crying and asking for news. Word arrived that a second assassin had stabbed Secretary Seward as he lay in his bed, badly wounding the statesman. Through the night Johnson received reports that Lincoln lay very close to death.

Abraham Lincoln on his deathbed

Early in the morning of April 15 Johnson solemnly walked with two bodyguards to the Petersen Boarding House across from Ford's Theater. People wept as the vice-president stepped along the narrow hallway and was ushered into the back bedroom. With his hat in his hand Johnson gazed at Lincoln's body stretched across the bed. He heard the president's struggled breathing and saw the blood-stained pillow beneath his head. It was obvious the wounded man could not survive. Taking the hand of the president's son Robert, he whispered a few words. In the Petersen parlor he silently grasped Mrs. Lincoln's hand. Then he sadly returned to his hotel room.

51

Secretary of War Edwin Stanton

At 7:22 A.M. Abraham Lincoln died. Standing at his
bedside, Secretary of War Edwin Stanton wept and declared, "Now he belongs to the ages." Mournful cabinet
members hastened to the Kirkwood House in a drizzling
rain. In the hotel parlor the group gravely gathered. Secretary of the Treasury McCulloch later recalled that Johnson
was "grief stricken like the rest . . . but he was neverthe-
less calm and self-possessed." At 10:00 A.M., Supreme
Court Chief Justice Salmon P. Chase arrived to administer
the presidential oath. Placing his hand upon a Bible, fifty-
six-year-old Johnson somberly swore "to preserve, protect
and defend the Constitution of the United States." Just
forty-one days after Andrew Johnson became vice-president, the tragic murder of Abraham Lincoln had thrust
him into the White House as seventeenth U.S. president.

Above: Andrew Johnson takes the oath of office in the Kirkwood House parlor.
Below: Officers planning the capture of John Wilkes Booth and David Herold

Chapter 5

The Constitution President

Bells tolled mournfully. Flags drooped at half-mast. Black crepe hung in windows and doorways. All of the North grieved over Abraham Lincoln's sudden death. Many people blamed the South for the horrible deed and demanded swift revenge against the southern states.

During the days following Lincoln's assassination, President Johnson felt this bitterness as deeply as anyone. Referring to the defeated Confederates he exclaimed, "I hold that . . . treason is a crime and crime must be punished. . . . Treason must be made infamous, and traitors must be impoverished." Punishment of the South had never been Abraham Lincoln's desire. For months he had fought with Congress over this issue. When Ohio senator Ben Wade heard Johnson's angry words he declared, "Johnson, we have faith in you. By the Gods, there will be no trouble now in running the government."

Opposite page: Lady Liberty, pardoning the rebels, wonders, "Shall I trust these men?"

55

On May 22, 1865, President Johnson stood on a platform erected in front of the White House. For hours he proudly watched as regiment after regiment of veteran Union soldiers paraded in a final grand review. Officers saluted as they trotted by on horseback. Bayonets glistened in the sunlight as enlisted men marched past. The crowds cheered and waved flags to honor the brave troops that had won the war.

That same month citizens jammed a Washington courtroom to witness the trial of the Lincoln conspirators. Already John Wilkes Booth was dead, shot when on April 25 soldiers surrounded the barn in which he was hiding near Bowling Green, Virginia.

Within days the Washington jury condemned four others to die as well. David Herold, Lewis Paine (Seward's attacker), and George Atzerodt grimly accepted their sentences.

Some people petitioned President Johnson to pardon Mrs. Mary Surratt, however. Mrs. Surratt had run the boardinghouse where Booth and his friends met to plot. Based on the evidence presented against her, President Johnson insisted the jury's verdict be carried out. On July 7 a Washington executioner dropped the gallows trap and all four dangled by their necks.

On May 11 Union cavalrymen captured Confederate president Jefferson Davis in Irwinsville, Georgia. Clapped in irons, the hated southern leader was imprisoned without trial at Fortress Monroe, Virginia. Two years of harsh treatment followed, until Davis was released on bail in 1867.

LEWIS PAYNE (PAINE) — 21
Unemployed
Hanged July 7, 1865
LIBRARY OF CONGRESS PHOTO

GEORGE ATZERODT — 30
Carriage Maker
Hanged July 7, 1865
LIBRARY OF CONGRESS PHOTO

DAVID E. HEROLD — 23
Drugstore Clerk
Hanged July 7, 1865
LIBRARY OF CONGRESS PHOTO

MARY E. SURRATT — 42
Boarding House Operator
Hanged July 7, 1865
MARGARET BEARDEN PHOTO

DR. SAMUEL MUDD — 32
Medical Doctor / Farmer
Life Imprisonment
LIBRARY OF CONGRESS PHOTO

SAMUEL ARNOLD — 28
Commissary Clerk
Life Imprisonment
LIBRARY OF CONGRESS PHOTO

MICHAEL O'LAUGHLIN — 28
Feedstore Clerk
Life Imprisonment
LIBRARY OF CONGRESS PHOTO

EDWARD SPANGLER — 40
Ford's Theatre Stagehand
Life Imprisonment
LIBRARY OF CONGRESS PHOTO

Above: Conspirators who were convicted in the plot to assassinate President Lincoln and other officials

Below: The capture of Jefferson Davis, president of the Confederate States of America, after the Civil War

Johnson's wife, Eliza (left), and daughter, Martha Johnson Patterson (right)

For two months after her husband's death, Mary Todd Lincoln remained in mourning at the White House. At last, in June 1865, she sadly left for home in Springfield, Illinois, and the Johnson family took possession of the whitewashed mansion. Years of poor health had left Eliza Johnson an invalid. The new First Lady spent most of her time resting in an upstairs room. To act as official White House hostess, Johnson invited his daughter, Mrs. Martha Patterson, as well as her family, to live with them. Mrs. Patterson performed her duties with simple charm and grace. To provide the family with fresh milk and butter, she bought two cows and grazed them on the White House lawn. "We are plain people from the mountains of Tennessee," she once explained, "called here for a short time by a national calamity. I trust too much will not be expected of us." With Johnson's loving family around him, the White House became a comfortable home.

Many of the beaten Confederate soldiers who returned home in the spring of 1865 found only sorrow and hardship. Crops had gone unplanted, and destroyed factories lay in smoky, tumbled heaps. On country roads, whites and blacks alike wandered about searching for employment. The Civil War had ruined the southern economy.

"With malice toward none, with charity for all . . . let us strive . . . to bind up the nation's wounds," Lincoln had asked in his second inaugural address. Following in Lincoln's footsteps, President Johnson soon understood the need to reunite the country smoothly. "I love the southern people," he revealed as he softened his vengeful attitude. "I know them to be brave and honorable, I know that they have accepted the situation and will come back into the Union in good faith." For the sake of the entire United States, Johnson determined to be a friend to the South during this period known as Reconstruction.

On May 29, 1865, Johnson made a startling proclamation: "To the end . . . that the authority of the government of the United States may be restored and that peace, order and freedom be established, I, Andrew Johnson, President of the United States, do . . . hereby grant to all persons who have . . . participated in the existing rebellion, amnesty and pardon. . . ." This general amnesty offered U.S. citizenship to almost all former Confederates willing to take an oath of national loyalty. Through the next months, hundreds of grateful southerners thronged the White House corridors each day seeking official pardons.

Johnson pardons rebels at the White House in 1865.

Out of the rubble of war the southern states struggled to rebuild their governments. Lincoln's Emancipation Proclamation in 1863 already had freed the slaves in the Confederate states. Now Johnson strongly urged that all state legislatures ratify a new amendment to the Constitution. This Thirteenth Amendment stated: "Neither slavery nor involuntary servitude . . . shall exist within the United States." Most southern states quickly followed Johnson's advice, although they also enacted "Black Codes" to restrict the former slaves. On December 18, 1865, the Thirteenth Amendment passed into law.

Through the summer and fall Johnson used his executive office to guide the nation through its troubled times.

A portrait of Andrew Johnson

On October 13 he happily declared, "We are making very rapid progress—so rapid I sometimes cannot realize it. It appears like a dream!" Many people praised Johnson's efforts to restore peace. "We can assure him," remarked the *New York Herald*, "that he is universally regarded . . . as the proper man for the crisis." A large number of northern politicians, however, deeply resented Johnson's power and his friendly attitude toward the beaten foe. Congress was in recess during these months, and anti-southern Republicans could only watch Johnson's progress with rage. "If something is not done," grumbled Congressman Thaddeus Stevens, "the President will be crowned King before the next Congress meets."

In December, the nation's senators and representatives finally gathered in session at the Capitol. In his first message to Congress Johnson hopefully stated, "It has been my steadfast object . . . to derive a healing policy from the fundamental and unchanging principles of the Constitution. . . . I know very well that this policy is attended with some risk. . . . But it is a risk that must be taken."

Northern Republicans turned a deaf ear to Johnson's words. They rudely refused to admit duly elected southerners into Congress. Instead they formed a special Joint Select Committee headed by Thaddeus Stevens to examine Johnson's Reconstruction policies. House Speaker Schuyler Colfax warned, "The duty of Congress is as plain as the sun's pathway in the Heavens; the door having been shut in the rebel faces, it is still to be kept bolted." Speaker Colfax, Representative Stevens, Ohio senator Ben Wade, Massachusetts senator Charles Sumner, and other northern Republicans demanded that the South be treated like a conquered foreign country. These men soon came to be called Radical Republicans. Ignoring the Constitution and the kind work of President Johnson, the Radical Republicans set upon a program to punish the South and further insure the rights of the newly freed blacks. "The Republican party and it alone can save the Union," sourly declared Thaddeus Stevens.

In February 1866, Congress passed the Freedmen's Bureau Act. This bill would provide southern blacks with educational help, medical services, farmland, and jobs. Unfortunately, the bill also would keep the southern states

The Primary School for Freedmen in Vicksburg, Mississippi, opened during Reconstruction

under U.S. military rule and deny southern whites many of their Constitutional rights. When the bill reached President Johnson's desk, he refused to sign it into law. Instead he returned a veto message to Congress. "The effect of this veto," remarked Navy Secretary Welles, "will probably be an open rupture between the President and a portion of the Republican members of Congress." In fact, the Radical Republicans angrily fumed at Johnson's power to block their desires. The Constitution required a two-thirds Senate vote to override a presidential veto, and such a thing rarely had been done in American history.

For the time being, the Radical Republicans were not strong enough to control Congress completely. While they awaited the next congressional elections, these politicians ridiculed Johnson in the press, calling him King Andy. "Andrew Johnson must learn," grimly remarked old Thaddeus Stevens, that "as Congress shall order he must obey." Repeatedly the Radicals passed unfair Reconstruction laws, but each time Johnson vetoed them. The president realized that the Radicals intended to ruin him and destroy his work. "The wicked rebel has been put down by the strong arm of the Government," he exclaimed, "but now another rebellion has started, a rebellion to overthrow the Constitution and revolutionize the Government."

Soon Johnson saw the need to appeal directly to the good nature of the northern people. On August 28, 1866, a locomotive belched smoke and chugged out of Washington station. The special train it pulled carried President Johnson, Secretary of State Seward, General Ulysses S. Grant, and other important officials on a "Swing Round the Circle." During this two-thousand-mile tour across the North, Johnson intended to speak in behalf of congressional candidates who supported his policies.

In Baltimore, Philadelphia, and New York huge crowds cheered the president. "I leave in your hands the Constitution and the Union," Johnson proclaimed, "and the glorious flag of your country not with twenty-five but with thirty-six stars." "I have been fighting the South and they have been whipped and crushed, and they acknowledge their defeat and accept the terms of the Constitution; and now as I go around the circle, having fought

Cartoons during Johnson's "Swing Round the Circle"

traitors at the South, I am prepared to fight traitors at the North." Mustering all his skills as an orator, Johnson did his best to sway the people to his side.

Hurriedly the Radical Republicans sought to ruin Johnson's tour. They planted hecklers in the crowds to interrupt the president with jeers. Republican newspaper articles twisted Johnson's words, and cartoons openly insulted him. Stubbornly President Johnson finished his tour, but the popular tide had turned against him. In November, Radical Republicans scored enough election victories to gain a two-thirds control of Congress at last.

Opposite page and above: Anti-Johnson cartoons

Chapter 6

Impeached!

"The fall elections have passed and the Radicals retain their strength in Congress," confided Navy Secretary Welles in his diary. "President Johnson was and is denounced as a traitor because he does not repel and persecute the beaten Rebels."

Gleefully the Radical Republicans thronged the halls of the Capitol, determined to rule the nation in spite of the president. During the early months of 1867 Congress hurriedly passed several new bills. Some of them genuinely helped southern blacks become better citizens. Others subjected southern whites to stern treatment. At the White House, President Johnson strove to separate the good bills from the bad and maintain the power and dignity of his office. While president, he would veto a total of twenty-nine bills, and Congress would in turn override fifteen of these vetoes.

Among the vetoed bills that the Radical Republicans managed to push through were four severe laws known as the Reconstruction Acts. These laws divided the South into five military districts commanded by U.S. Army generals. States could apply for readmission to the Union only if they met certain Congressional guidelines. The former slaves could vote, but many white men were refused the right.

To further protect blacks, the southern states were required to ratify the new Fourteenth Amendment. This declared that federal laws protecting citizens were more important than state laws, and that no state could "deprive any person of life, liberty or property, without due process of the laws."

In the months ahead, northern politicians carrying luggage fashioned from carpet material swarmed into the South to run the local governments. These "carpetbaggers" were often corrupt, openly buying the support of black voters and robbing state treasuries.

Ex-Confederates angrily searched for ways to regain control of their states. Soon a secret organization called the Ku Klux Klan rose up throughout the South. Disguised in ghostly robes and high peaked hoods, Klansmen nightly galloped across the countryside. Burning houses and brutally attacking their enemies, they struck terror into the hearts of black voters and carpetbaggers alike.

To combat the violence, U.S. cavalrymen stepped up their patrols. The national peace envisioned by presidents Lincoln and Johnson had turned into a southern nightmare that would last for many years.

Stubbornly Johnson continued battling with Congress. Each of his veto messages presented his views in thoughtful, effective language. Soon the Radical Republicans sought a way to rid themselves of Johnson completely. Some congressmen spread ugly rumors that Johnson had conspired with John Wilkes Booth to murder Abraham Lincoln. The House Judiciary Committee started an investigation to learn if Johnson were guilty of any crimes. To insult him further, Congress passed over Johnson's veto the Tenure of Office Act. That law forbade the president to remove from office certain federal workers without the consent of the Senate.

President Johnson suffered many of Congress's insults and slanders quietly, but the Tenure of Office Act enraged him. It clearly was unconstitutional, for it interfered with his executive powers as president. At cabinet meetings Secretary of War Edwin Stanton often disagreed with Johnson. Secretly Stanton was helping the Radical Republicans. "It is impossible," exclaimed Johnson, "to get along with such a man in such a position, and I can stand it no longer." In August 1867 Johnson finally removed the disloyal secretary from office. In his place, he appointed the heroic general Ulysses S. Grant.

For five months Grant served as Secretary of War. Grant wished to win the Republican presidential nomination in 1868, however. The Radicals advised him that he could improve his chances if he helped them. Grant resigned his office in February 1868 and returned the position to Stanton. Before long the bearded, bespectacled Stanton barricaded himself in his room at the War Department.

Above: Johnson and Ulysses S. Grant discuss the Tenure of Office Act.
Below: A cartoon showing Johnson wounded by daggers of opposition

Johnson is served with a summons for his impeachment trial.

Furiously, Johnson again ordered Stanton's removal. Instead he appointed General Lorenzo Thomas as War Secretary. Johnson's continued defiance of the Tenure of Office Act played directly into the hands of the Radical Republicans. "Didn't I tell you so?" exclaimed Thaddeus Stevens. "If you don't kill the beast it will kill you."

On February 24, 1868, uproar reigned in the House of Representatives. Members called Johnson "a disgrace to this great and glorious age" and "the great criminal of our . . . country." At five o'clock in the afternoon, by a count of 126 to 47, they voted that Andrew Johnson be impeached for "high crimes and misdemeanors." This declaration meant that Johnson would have to stand trial in the Senate. If convicted of breaking the law, he would be shamefully removed from office. Stunned visitors rushed from the galleries to spread the news. In American history no president ever had been impeached before.

Supreme Court Chief Justice Salmon P. Chase

The House presented eleven separate articles of impeachment against Johnson, eight of which charged that he had conspired to violate the Constitution. "Impeach me for violating the Constitution!" Johnson exploded when he heard this news. "Damn them! Haven't I been struggling ever since I have been in this chair to uphold the Constitution they trample under foot!" Navy Secretary Welles called the eleven articles "a mountain of words, but not even a mouse of impeachable material. . . . Those who may vote to convict . . . would as readily vote to impeach the President had he been accused of stepping on a dog's tail."

On March 13, 1865, scores of gentlemen and ladies, diplomats, and friends of congressmen presented special tickets and gained admittance into the Senate galleries. The trial of Andrew Johnson was about to begin. Black-robed Supreme Court Chief Justice Chase was about to preside. The fifty-four members of the Senate made up the jury. A two-thirds majority—thirty-six votes—would be needed for conviction.

The seven prosecutors in Johnson's impeachment case

"Hear ye! Hear ye!" echoed the voice of the Senate's sergeant-at-arms as he brought the chamber to order. The senators were sworn to do their duty. The impeachment articles were described. Then the Senate voted to give Johnson's lawyers only nine days to prepare a defense.

On March 23, 1868, the trial began. Seven House members, called managers, prosecuted the case against the president. Day after day they presented evidence and questioned witnesses. They demanded Johnson be convicted for defying the Tenure of Office Act. The president's lawyers defended him as well as they could, but the senators sometimes refused to hear their evidence.

Through April and into May the exciting trial gripped the nation. With dignity President Johnson never once attended the proceedings. Instead he waited calmly at the White House. When his servant, Warden, returned from the trial each evening, Johnson would cheerfully ask, "Well, Warden, what are the signs of the zodiac to-day?"

A cartoon wrongly predicting Johnson's farewell to the presidency

At last the trial neared its sensational end. The House managers had presented a weak case based on hatred and emotions. During the closing arguments against Johnson, Manager George S. Boutwell warned, "By his acquittal you surrender the government into the hands of an usurping and unscrupulous man. . . ." Defense lawyer Thomas Nelson countered, "It almost shocks me to think that the President of the United States is to be dragged out of his office on these miserable little questions. . . ."

On May 7 the Senate adjourned to deliberate. As each senator weighed the evidence against Johnson, the power of the presidency and the future of the country lay in the balance. During the tense days that followed, newspaper writers tried to influence the senators' decisions. The *New York Tribune* wrote: "He is an aching tooth in the national jaw, a screeching infant in a crowded lecture-room, and there can be no peace nor comfort till he is out."

The nine Democrats and three conservative Republicans in the Senate sided with President Johnson. Of the other Republican senators, the Radicals could count upon thirty-five sure votes. Of the seven undecided Republican senators, the Radicals needed only one man to convict the president. Intensely pressured, Republican senator James Grimes of Iowa suffered a stroke that left him partially paralyzed. Still he bravely announced his decision to vote for acquittal. Others also scorned the threats of the Radicals and vowed to vote the president innocent.

Only one senator remained undecided. Frantically the Radicals fixed their attention upon Senator Edmund G. Ross of Kansas. They pestered him, attempted to bribe him, and hired detectives to shadow his every move. On the night before the Senate's vote, Ross received a telegram from his home state. "Kansas has heard the evidence and demands the conviction of the President. (signed) D. R. Anthony and 1,000 others." All the nation anxiously waited to hear from the silent senator.

The day of judgment arrived on May 16, 1868. At the Capitol the court convened, with Chief Justice Chase presiding. Crowds jammed the Senate chamber, the galleries, and corridors outside. Every Senate chair was filled; even sickly Senator Grimes had been carried in to vote.

"The Clerk will now call the roll," ordered Chief Justice Chase. "Is the respondent, Andrew Johnson, President of the United States, guilty or not guilty of a high misdemeanor as charged. . . ." One by one the senators stood and recorded their votes. Each voted as he had promised, so that only Edmund Ross's vote really mattered now.

"Mr. Senator Ross," questioned Chief Justice Chase at last, "how say you?"

Quietly Ross rose from his seat and gazed about the chamber. "Every individual in that great audience," he later recalled, "seemed distinctly visible. . . . Every fan was folded, not a foot moved, not the rustle of a garment, not a whisper was heard. . . . Hope and fear seemed blended in every face."

As Ross thought about his political future among the Republicans he realized, "I almost literally looked down into my open grave." Still he bravely followed his best judgment.

Andrew Johnson was innocent. The Radicals had lost their case by the closest possible margin.

Colonel William Crook, the president's bodyguard, sprang down the Capitol steps and ran along Washington's Pennsylvania Avenue. Out of breath, he rushed inside the White House and found Johnson seated with some friends in the library.

"Mr. President," he cried out, "you are acquitted." Everyone jumped up to congratulate Johnson. Tears of thanks rolled down his face as he shook their hands.

Crook next hurried upstairs to Eliza Johnson's room. After knocking, he entered and found the frail First Lady sewing in her rocking chair. "He's acquitted," joyfully exclaimed the devoted servant. "The President is acquitted." Rising from her seat, Mrs. Johnson weakly clasped his hand. "Crook," she gladly sighed, "I knew he would be acquitted; I knew it."

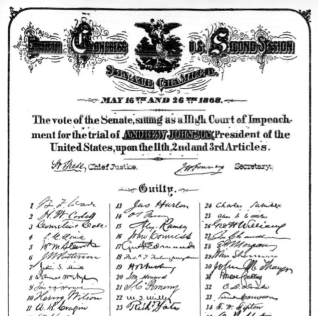

Left: The vote of the Senate in Johnson's trial
Above: Senator Ross, who broke the tie
Below: Friends congratulating Johnson

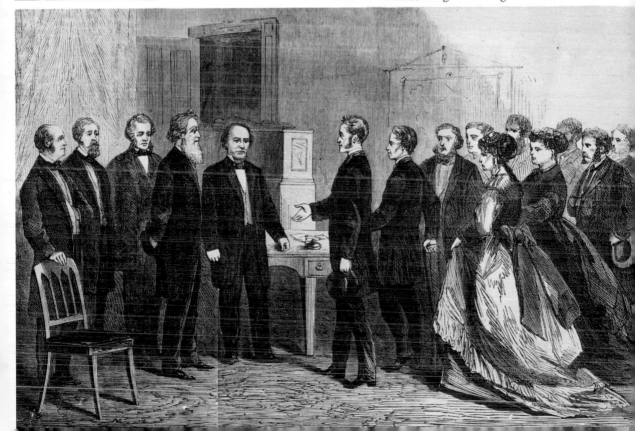

Chapter 7

Lasting Triumphs

"It is a victory not for myself but for the Constitution and the country," exclaimed Johnson following his impeachment trial. Secure in the presidency, he sternly continued his battle with Congress, vetoing bills he thought unfair. Many northerners hated him for it. "Everybody misunderstands me," he told William Crook one day. "I am not trying to introduce anything new. I am only trying to carry out the measures toward the South that Mr. Lincoln would have done had he lived." In the South, people grew to respect Johnson for his gallant efforts. Ex-governor Zebulon Vance of North Carolina declared, "Through Andrew Johnson, and such as he, we begin to see how it is possible to love our whole country once more."

While the United States struggled to heal itself, Johnson's administration did experience some successes. In 1867 Nebraska proudly joined the Union. As the nation's thirty-seventh state, it soon attracted new settlers to its fertile soil.

In camps along the Texas border in 1867, U.S. soldiers gazed across the Rio Grande at Mexico. The Monroe Doctrine of 1823 had warned European powers not to encroach upon countries in the Western Hemisphere. During the Civil War, however, France had installed Austrian Archduke Maximilian as ruler of Mexico. Only when Johnson threatened war did the French agree to withdraw. Nobly, Maximilian remained without French support, but Mexican nationalists soon captured the false king and stood him before a firing squad.

In the spring of 1867, Secretary of State William Seward scored a remarkable achievement. One night the Russian ambassador arrived at Seward's home with an offer from his czar. The Russian ruler was willing to sell the territory he possessed on North America's Alaskan peninsula. Seward immediately jumped at the opportunity. He agreed upon a price of $7,200,000 for the vast northern region of over 500,000 square miles. Seward realized the immense value of Alaska's long coastline, good harbors, and untold natural resources.

Many congressmen insisted that $7,200,000 was too much to pay for miles of rocks and ice. "Walrussia," they called it, the Russian land of walruses. Critics quickly dubbed the purchase "Seward's Folly." Newspaper cartoons teased about "Seward's Icebox" and "Johnson's polar bear garden." Seward wisely continued to push for the purchase, however, and Congress finally voted the money in April 1867. Alaska became U.S. territory and, in the years that followed, grateful Americans grew to recognize the tremendous worth of their investment.

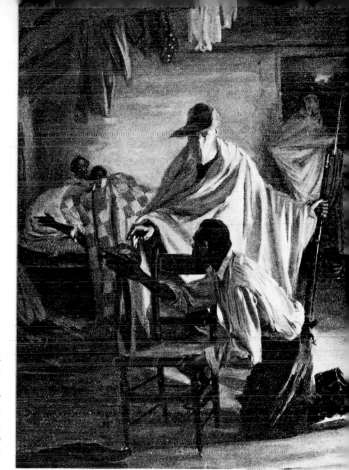

**Right: The Ku Klux Klan
terrorizing a black man**

**Below: A cartoon ridiculing
the purchase of Alaska from
Russia. Alaska, also known
as "Russian America," is
shown as simply a huge block
of ice costing $7,200,000.**

Ulysses S. Grant,
eighteenth president
of the United States

As the national election year of 1868 arrived, Johnson understood his chances of winning a presidential nomination were slim. At their May convention in Chicago, cheering Republicans excitedly nominated Ulysses S. Grant on the first ballot. Democratic delegates gathered six weeks later at New York City. Although Johnson received some support in the early balloting, the Democrats finally picked New York governor Horatio Seymour as their candidate. From the White House Johnson watched the fall campaign with disappointment. He offered no comment when on November 3, 1868, Americans elected Ulysses S. Grant as eighteenth United States president.

During the months that remained in his term, Johnson worked as hard as ever to protect the Constitution and heal the nation. On Christmas Day, 1868, he extended his southern pardon to include former Confederate leaders. Even Jefferson Davis would avoid standing trial now.

At last, on March 4, 1869, came inauguration day. When the cabinet members arrived at the White House that morning, they eagerly expected to attend the inauguration ceremony. Seward pointedly asked if everyone were ready, but Johnson silently kept working at his desk. "Will we not be late?" asked Seward. "Ought we not to start immediately?" Quietly Johnson looked up and answered, "I am inclined to think that we will finish up our work here by ourselves."

Through the morning sixty-year-old Johnson remained at the White House, clearing his desk. Just after noon, while crowds at the Capitol cheered Grant, Johnson shook hands with his cabinet and departed with his family from the White House forever. The Johnsons' years in Washington had been turbulent, but they had brought no shame to the White House. With feeling, Secretary Welles remarked, "Socially and personally I part with them with regret; no better persons have occupied the executive mansion."

After an absence of eight long years, Johnson looked forward to returning to Greeneville. During his journey home, southerners greeted him differently than they had at the start of the Civil War. When his train stopped in Lynchburg, Virginia, instead of putting a rope around his neck, a crowd loudly cheered him now. Eight years earlier in Greeneville, as Johnson fled the town, a banner lettered "Andrew Johnson, Traitor" had been stretched across Main Street. Now as he proudly approached his town a different banner hung there reading, "Welcome Home, Andrew Johnson, Patriot."

The Johnson home, used during the war as a barrack and later as a hospital, required immediate repairs. A visiting *New York Herald* reporter declared, "The fences of the lot and windows of the house show evident signs of dilapidation." The Johnsons set to work sweeping out dust and cobwebs while workmen puttied windows. Soon the house was livable again, and Johnson quickly turned his attention to politics. Full of fire, he was determined to prove that his actions as president had been right. "I was impeached," he exclaimed, "and while legally vindicated, yet by a minority vote. I would rather have the vindication of my state by electing me to my old seat in the Senate of the United States than to be monarch of the grandest empire on earth. . . ."

In 1869 and again in 1872 Johnson campaigned hard for Congress. Although he lost both times, the ex-president showed himself to be a strictly honorable man. These years were a time of embarrassing national corruption. Johnson claimed that President Grant's cabinet, for example, "was a sort of lottery, those getting the best places that paid the most." Offices were being "disposed of at various prices from $65,000 down to a box of segars." Crookedness in the War Department, the Interior Department, the Post Office, the Navy Department, and also among members of Congress deeply blackened Grant's administration.

In January 1875, Johnson campaigned again to win a Senate seat. This time, after intense balloting, the Tennessee legislature wisely chose Andrew Johnson to represent the state in Washington. News of Johnson's victory received national notice. No ex-president ever had

Andrew Johnson of Tennessee returns to the U.S. Senate in 1875.

returned to serve in the U.S. Senate. "We shall not be sorry to see him again in public life," trumpeted the *New York Times.* "Whatever his faults as President may have been, at any rate he went out of the White House as poor as he entered it and that is something to say in these times." The *New York Herald* declared, "He is the best man Tennessee could have chosen. . . . The Senate needs men who have the courage to speak the truth. . . ."

Time had revealed the unselfishness of Johnson's character. "I will go to the Senate," he proudly announced, "with no personal hostility toward any one. . . . My few remaining years shall be devoted to the . . . prosperity of my country which I love more than my own life."

On March 6, 1875, the sturdy old man stepped slowly through the Capitol rotunda and into the U.S. Senate chamber. The room fell silent as the ex-president gazed around. It was here that just seven years earlier his reputation had suffered unheard-of attacks during his impeachment trial.

In a moment, applause broke out in the galleries. Senate friends and also former enemies gathered around to shake his hand. He found his desk covered with flowers, and a page soon presented him with another fragrant garland. Tearfully Johnson acknowledged his "welcome home."

"The only way to fight error," he had once exclaimed, "is to strike it a direct blow. Hit it between the eyes, and drop it to its knees. . . ." During the few days that the Senate remained in session, Johnson bluntly attacked the corruption of the Grant administration and the failure of its Reconstruction program. "Let peace and union be restored to the land," he forcefully insisted.

At the end of March Johnson journeyed back to Greeneville. At sixty-six years of age, the tailor-politician needed a restful vacation. On July 27, 1875, Johnson traveled over to Carter County to visit at the farm of his daughter, Mary Stover. In the afternoon he sat in his guest room chatting with his little granddaughter, Lillie. As the child turned to leave, she heard a sudden crash. Her grandfather had toppled forward and lay sprawled helplessly across the carpet. The victim of a stroke, his left side was totally paralyzed.

Gently his family placed him in bed. Through the next thirty-six hours he calmly talked of his life and political

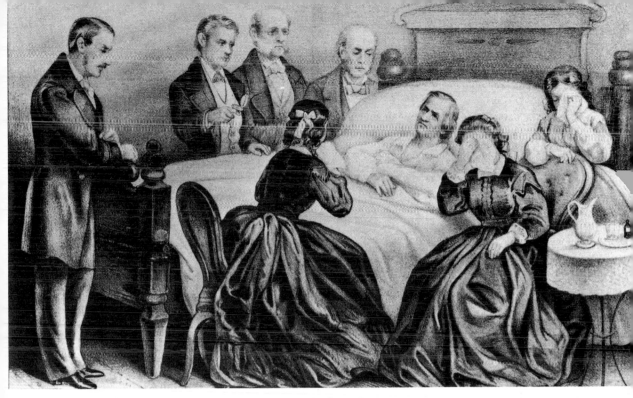

The death of Andrew Johnson

career. When a second stroke thrust him into unconsciousness, the family sadly realized there was no hope. At about 2:00 A.M. on July 31, 1875, Andrew Johnson died.

Common Tennesseans deeply mourned the loss of the man who always had fought in their behalf. In time, all of the nation would more fully realize Johnson's worth.

Friends and relatives sorrowfully transported his body back to Greeneville. There the words of one of Johnson's famous speeches echoed in many people's ears. "When I die," he had declared, "I desire no better winding sheet than the Stars and Stripes, and no softer pillow than the Constitution of my country." On a hill overlooking Greeneville, Johnson was granted his wish. Wrapped in a U.S. flag, the old patriot was buried. Beneath his head rested a copy of the Constitution, the document he had defended so well throughout his noble life.

Chronology of American History

(Shaded area covers events in Andrew Johnson's lifetime.)

About A.D. 982—Eric the Red, born in Norway, reaches Greenland in one of the first European voyages to North America.

About 1000—Leif Ericson (Eric the Red's son) leads what is thought to be the first European expedition to mainland North America; Leif probably lands in Canada.

1492—Christopher Columbus, seeking a sea route from Spain to the Far East, discovers the New World.

1497—John Cabot reaches Canada in the first English voyage to North America.

1513—Ponce de Léon explores Florida in search of the fabled Fountain of Youth.

1519-1521—Hernando Cortés of Spain conquers Mexico.

1534—French explorers led by Jacques Cartier enter the Gulf of St. Lawrence in Canada.

1540—Spanish explorer Francisco Coronado begins exploring the American Southwest, seeking the riches of the mythical Seven Cities of Cibola.

1565—St. Augustine, Florida, the first permanent European town in what is now the United States, is founded by the Spanish.

1607—Jamestown, Virginia, is founded, the first permanent English town in the present-day U.S.

1608—Frenchman Samuel de Champlain founds the village of Quebec, Canada.

1609—Henry Hudson explores the eastern coast of present-day U.S. for the Netherlands; the Dutch then claim parts of New York, New Jersey, Delaware, and Connecticut and name the area New Netherland.

1619—The English colonies' first shipment of black slaves arrives in Jamestown.

1620—English Pilgrims found Massachusetts' first permanent town at Plymouth.

1621—Massachusetts Pilgrims and Indians hold the famous first Thanksgiving feast in colonial America.

1623—Colonization of New Hampshire is begun by the English.

1624—Colonization of present-day New York State is begun by the Dutch at Fort Orange (Albany).

1625—The Dutch start building New Amsterdam (now New York City).

1630—The town of Boston, Massachusetts, is founded by the English Puritans.

1633—Colonization of Connecticut is begun by the English.

1634—Colonization of Maryland is begun by the English.

1636—Harvard, the colonies' first college, is founded in Massachusetts. Rhode Island colonization begins when Englishman Roger Williams founds Providence.

1638—Delaware colonization begins as Swedes build Fort Christina at present-day Wilmington.

1640—Stephen Daye of Cambridge, Massachusetts prints *The Bay Psalm Book*, the first English-language book published in what is now the U.S.

1643—Swedish settlers begin colonizing Pennsylvania.

About 1650—North Carolina is colonized by Virginia settlers.

1660—New Jersey colonization is begun by the Dutch at present-day Jersey City.

1670—South Carolina colonization is begun by the English near Charleston.

1673—Jacques Marquette and Louis Jolliet explore the upper Mississippi River for France.

1682—Philadelphia, Pennsylvania, is settled. La Salle explores Mississippi River all the way to its mouth in Louisiana and claims the whole Mississippi Valley for France.

1693—College of William and Mary is founded in Williamsburg, Virginia.

1700—Colonial population is about 250,000.

1703—Benjamin Franklin is born in Boston.

1732—George Washington, first president of the U.S., is born in Westmoreland County, Virginia.

1733—James Oglethorpe founds Savannah, Georgia; Georgia is established as the thirteenth colony.

1735—John Adams, second president of the U.S., is born in Braintree, Massachusetts.

1737—William Byrd founds Richmond, Virginia.

1738—British troops are sent to Georgia over border dispute with Spain.

1739—Black insurrection takes place in South Carolina.

1740—English Parliament passes act allowing naturalization of immigrants to American colonies after seven-year residence.

1743—Thomas Jefferson is born in Albemarle County, Virginia. Benjamin Franklin retires at age thirty-seven to devote himself to scientific inquiries and public service.

1744—King George's War begins; France joins war effort against England.

1745—During King George's War, France raids settlements in Maine and New York.

1747—Classes begin at Princeton College in New Jersey.

1748—The Treaty of Aix-la-Chapelle concludes King George's War.

1749—Parliament legally recognizes slavery in colonies and the inauguration of the plantation system in the South. George Washington becomes the surveyor for Culpepper County in Virginia.

1750—Thomas Walker passes through and names Cumberland Gap on his way toward Kentucky region. Colonial population is about 1,200,000.

1751—James Madison, fourth president of the U.S., is born in Port Conway, Virginia. English Parliament passes Currency Act, banning New England colonies from issuing paper money. George Washington travels to Barbados.

1752—Pennsylvania Hospital, the first general hospital in the colonies, is founded in Philadelphia. Benjamin Franklin uses a kite in a thunderstorm to demonstrate that lightning is a form of electricity.

1753—George Washington delivers command that the French withdraw from the Ohio River Valley; French disregard the demand. Colonial population is about 1,328,000.

1754—French and Indian War begins (extends to Europe as the Seven Years' War). Washington surrenders at Fort Necessity.

1755—French and Indians ambush Braddock. Washington becomes commander of Virginia troops.

1756—England declares war on France.

1758—James Monroe, fifth president of the U.S., is born in Westmoreland County, Virginia.

1759—Cherokee Indian war begins in southern colonies; hostilities extend to 1761. George Washington marries Martha Dandridge Custis.

1760—George III becomes king of England. Colonial population is about 1,600,000.

1762—England declares war on Spain.

1763—Treaty of Paris concludes the French and Indian War and the Seven Years' War. England gains Canada and most other French lands east of the Mississippi River.

1764—British pass the Sugar Act to gain tax money from the colonists. The issue of taxation without representation is first introduced in Boston. John Adams marries Abigail Smith.

1765—Stamp Act goes into effect in the colonies. Business virtually stops as almost all colonists refuse to use the stamps.

1766—British repeal the Stamp Act.

1767—John Quincy Adams, sixth president of the U.S. and son of second president John Adams, is born in Braintree, Massachusetts. Andrew Jackson, seventh president of the U.S., is born in Waxhaw settlement, South Carolina.

1769—Daniel Boone sights the Kentucky Territory.

1770—In the Boston Massacre, British soldiers kill five colonists and injure six. Townshend Acts are repealed, thus eliminating all duties on imports to the colonies except tea.

1771—Benjamin Franklin begins his autobiography, a work that he will never complete. The North Carolina assembly passes the "Bloody Act," which makes rioters guilty of treason.

1772—Samuel Adams rouses colonists to consider British threats to self-government.

1773—English Parliament passes the Tea Act. Colonists dressed as Mohawk Indians board British tea ships and toss 342 casks of tea into the water in what becomes known as the Boston Tea Party. William Henry Harrison is born in Charles City County, Virginia.

1774—British close the port of Boston to punish the city for the Boston Tea Party. First Continental Congress convenes in Philadelphia.

1775—American Revolution begins with battles of Lexington and Concord, Massachusetts. Second Continental Congress opens in Philadelphia. George Washington becomes commander-in-chief of the Continental army.

1776—Declaration of Independence is adopted on July 4.

1777—Congress adopts the American flag with thirteen stars and thirteen stripes. John Adams is sent to France to negotiate peace treaty.

1778—France declares war against Great Britain and becomes U.S. ally.

1779—British surrender to Americans at Vincennes. Thomas Jefferson is elected governor of Virginia. James Madison is elected to the Continental Congress.

1780—Benedict Arnold, first American traitor, defects to the British.

1781—Articles of Confederation go into effect. Cornwallis surrenders to George Washington at Yorktown, ending the American Revolution.

1782—American commissioners, including John Adams, sign peace treaty with British in Paris. Thomas Jefferson's wife, Martha, dies. Martin Van Buren is born in Kinderhook, New York.

1784—Zachary Taylor is born near Barboursville, Virginia.

1785—Congress adopts the dollar as the unit of currency. John Adams is made minister to Great Britain. Thomas Jefferson is appointed minister to France.

1786—Shays's Rebellion begins in Massachusetts.

1787—Constitutional Convention assembles in Philadelphia, with George Washington presiding; U.S. Constitution is adopted. Delaware, New Jersey, and Pennsylvania become states.

1788—Virginia, South Carolina, New York, Connecticut, New Hampshire, Maryland, and Massachusetts become states. U.S. Constitution is ratified. New York City is declared U.S. capital.

1789—Presidential electors elect George Washington and John Adams as first president and vice-president. Thomas Jefferson is appointed secretary of state. North Carolina becomes a state. French Revolution begins.

1790—Supreme Court meets for the first time. Rhode Island becomes a state. First national census in the U.S. counts 3,929,214 persons. John Tyler is born in Charles City County, Virginia.

1791—Vermont enters the Union. U.S. Bill of Rights, the first ten amendments to the Constitution, goes into effect. District of Columbia is established. James Buchanan is born in Stony Batter, Pennsylvania.

1792—Thomas Paine publishes *The Rights of Man*. Kentucky becomes a state. Two political parties are formed in the U.S., Federalist and Republican. Washington is elected to a second term, with Adams as vice-president.

1793—War between France and Britain begins; U.S. declares neutrality. Eli Whitney invents the cotton gin; cotton production and slave labor increase in the South.

1794—Eleventh Amendment to the Constitution is passed, limiting federal courts' power. "Whiskey Rebellion" in Pennsylvania protests federal whiskey tax. James Madison marries Dolley Payne Todd.

1795—George Washington signs the Jay Treaty with Great Britain. Treaty of San Lorenzo, between U.S. and Spain, settles Florida boundary and gives U.S. right to navigate the Mississippi. James Polk is born near Pineville, North Carolina.

1796—Tennessee enters the Union. Washington gives his Farewell Address, refusing a third presidential term. John Adams is elected president and Thomas Jefferson vice-president.

1797—Adams recommends defense measures against possible war with France. Napoleon Bonaparte and his army march against Austrians in Italy. U.S. population is about 4,900,000.

1798—Washington is named commander-in-chief of the U.S. Army. Department of the Navy is created. Alien and Sedition Acts are passed. Napoleon's troops invade Egypt and Switzerland.

1799—George Washington dies at Mount Vernon, New York. James Monroe is elected governor of Virginia. French Revolution ends. Napoleon becomes ruler of France.

1800—Thomas Jefferson and Aaron Burr tie for president. U.S. capital is moved from Philadelphia to Washington, D.C. The White House is built as presidents' home. Spain returns Louisiana to France. Millard Fillmore is born in Locke, New York.

1801—After thirty-six ballots, House of Representatives elects Thomas Jefferson president, making Burr vice-president. James Madison is named secretary of state.

1802—Congress abolishes excise taxes. U.S. Military Academy is founded at West Point, New York.

1803—Ohio enters the Union. Louisiana Purchase treaty is signed with France, greatly expanding U.S. territory.

1804—Twelfth Amendment to the Constitution rules that president and vice-president be elected separately. Alexander Hamilton is killed by Vice-President Aaron Burr in a duel. Orleans Territory is established. Napoleon crowns himself emperor of France. Franklin Pierce is born in Hillsborough Lower Village, New Hampshire.

1805—Thomas Jefferson begins his second term as president. Lewis and Clark expedition reaches the Pacific Ocean.

1806—Coinage of silver dollars is stopped; resumes in 1836.

1807—Aaron Burr is acquitted in treason trial. Embargo Act closes U.S. ports to trade.

1808—James Madison is elected president. Congress outlaws importing slaves from Africa. Andrew Johnson is born in Raleigh, North Carolina.

1809—Abraham Lincoln is born near Hodgenville, Kentucky.

1810—U.S. population is 7,240,000.

1811—William Henry Harrison defeats Indians at Tippecanoe. Monroe is named secretary of state.

1812—Louisiana becomes a state. U.S. declares war on Britain (War of 1812). James Madison is reelected president. Napoleon invades Russia.

1813—British forces take Fort Niagara and Buffalo, New York.

1814—Francis Scott Key writes "The Star-Spangled Banner." British troops burn much of Washington, D.C., including the White House. Treaty of Ghent ends War of 1812. James Monroe becomes secretary of war.

1815—Napoleon meets his final defeat at Battle of Waterloo.

1816—James Monroe is elected president. Indiana becomes a state.

1817—Mississippi becomes a state. Construction on Erie Canal begins.

1818—Illinois enters the Union. The present thirteen-stripe flag is adopted. Border between U.S. and Canada is agreed upon.

1819—Alabama becomes a state. U.S. purchases Florida from Spain. Thomas Jefferson establishes the University of Virginia.

1820—James Monroe is reelected. In the Missouri Compromise, Maine enters the Union as a free (non-slave) state.

1821—Missouri enters the Union as a slave state. Santa Fe Trail opens the American Southwest. Mexico declares independence from Spain. Napoleon Bonaparte dies.

1822—U.S. recognizes Mexico and Colombia. Liberia in Africa is founded as a home for freed slaves. Ulysses S. Grant is born in Point Pleasant, Ohio. Rutherford B. Hayes is born in Delaware, Ohio.

1823—Monroe Doctrine closes North and South America to European colonizing or invasion.

1824—House of Representatives elects John Quincy Adams president when none of the four candidates wins a majority in national election. Mexico becomes a republic.

1825—Erie Canal is opened. U.S. population is 11,300,000.

1826—Thomas Jefferson and John Adams both die on July 4, the fiftieth anniversary of the Declaration of Independence.

1828—Andrew Jackson is elected president. Tariff of Abominations is passed, cutting imports.

1829—James Madison attends Virginia's constitutional convention. Slavery is abolished in Mexico. Chester A. Arthur is born in Fairfield, Vermont.

1830—Indian Removal Act to resettle Indians west of the Mississippi is approved.

1831—James Monroe dies in New York City. James A. Garfield is born in Orange, Ohio. Cyrus McCormick develops his reaper.

1832—Andrew Jackson, nominated by the new Democratic Party, is reelected president.

1833—Britain abolishes slavery in its colonies. Benjamin Harrison is born in North Bend, Ohio.

1835—Federal government becomes debt-free for the first time.

1836—Martin Van Buren becomes president. Texas wins independence from Mexico. Arkansas joins the Union. James Madison dies at Montpelier, Virginia.

1837—Michigan enters the Union. U.S. population is 15,900,000. Grover Cleveland is born in Caldwell, New Jersey.

1840—William Henry Harrison is elected president.

1841—President Harrison dies in Washington, D.C., one month after inauguration. Vice-President John Tyler succeeds him.

1843—William McKinley is born in Niles, Ohio.

1844—James Knox Polk is elected president. Samuel Morse sends first telegraphic message.

1845—Texas and Florida become states. Potato famine in Ireland causes massive emigration from Ireland to U.S. Andrew Jackson dies near Nashville, Tennessee.

1846—Iowa enters the Union. War with Mexico begins.

1847—U.S. captures Mexico City.

1848—Zachary Taylor becomes president. Treaty of Guadalupe Hidalgo ends Mexico-U.S. war. Wisconsin becomes a state.

1849—James Polk dies in Nashville, Tennessee.

1850—President Taylor dies in Washington, D.C.; Vice-President Millard Fillmore succeeds him. California enters the Union, breaking tie between slave and free states.

1852—Franklin Pierce is elected president.

1853—Gadsden Purchase transfers Mexican territory to U.S.

1854—"War for Bleeding Kansas" is fought between slave and free states.

1855—Czar Nicholas I of Russia dies, succeeded by Alexander II.

1856—James Buchanan is elected president. In Massacre of Potawatomi Creek, Kansas-slavers are murdered by free-staters. Woodrow Wilson is born in Staunton, Pennsylvania.

1857—William Howard Taft is born in Cincinnati, Ohio.

1858—Minnesota enters the Union. Theodore Roosevelt is born in New York City.

1859—Oregon becomes a state.

1860—Abraham Lincoln is elected president. South Carolina secedes from the Union in protest.

1861—Arkansas, Tennessee, North Carolina, and Virginia secede. Kansas enters the Union as a free state. Civil War begins.

1862—Union forces capture Fort Henry, Roanoke Island, Fort Donelson, Jacksonville, and New Orleans; Union armies are defeated at the battles of Bull Run and Fredericksburg. Martin Van Buren dies in Kinderhook, New York. John Tyler dies near Charles City, Virginia.

1863—Lincoln issues Emancipation Proclamation: all slaves held in rebelling territories are declared free. West Virginia becomes a state.

1864—Abraham Lincoln is reelected. Nevada becomes a state.

1865—Lincoln is assassinated in Washington, D.C., and succeeded by Andrew Johnson. U.S. Civil War ends on May 26. Thirteenth Amendment abolishes slavery. Warren G. Harding is born in Blooming Grove, Ohio.

1867—Nebraska becomes a state. U.S. buys Alaska from Russia for $7,200,000. Reconstruction Acts are passed.

1868—President Johnson is impeached for violating Tenure of Office Act, but is acquitted by Senate. Ulysses S. Grant is elected president. Fourteenth Amendment prohibits voting discrimination. James Buchanan dies in Lancaster, Pennsylvania.

1869—Franklin Pierce dies in Concord, New Hampshire.

1870—Fifteenth Amendment gives blacks the right to vote.

1872—Grant is reelected over Horace Greeley. General Amnesty Act pardons ex-Confederates. Calvin Coolidge is born in Plymouth Notch, Vermont.

1874—Millard Fillmore dies in Buffalo, New York. Herbert Hoover is born in West Branch, Iowa.

1875—Andrew Johnson dies in Carter's Station, Tennessee.

1876—Colorado enters the Union. "Custer's last stand": he and his men are massacred by Sioux Indians at Little Big Horn, Montana.

1877—Rutherford B. Hayes is elected president as all disputed votes are awarded to him.

1880—James A. Garfield is elected president.

1881—President Garfield is assassinated and dies in Elberon, New Jersey. Vice-President Chester A. Arthur succeeds him.

1882—U.S. bans Chinese immigration. Franklin D. Roosevelt is born in Hyde Park, New York.

1885—Ulysses S. Grant dies in Mount McGregor, New York.

1886—Statue of Liberty is dedicated. Chester A. Arthur dies in New York City.

1888—Benjamin Harrison is elected president.

1889—North Dakota, South Dakota, Washington, and Montana become states.

1890—Dwight D. Eisenhower is born in Denison, Texas. Idaho and Wyoming become states.

1892—Grover Cleveland is elected president.

1893—Rutherford B. Hayes dies in Fremont, Ohio.

1896—William McKinley is elected president. Utah becomes a state.

1898—U.S. declares war on Spain over Cuba.

1899—Philippines demand independence from U.S.

1900—McKinley is reelected. Boxer Rebellion against foreigners in China begins.

1901—McKinley is assassinated by anarchist Leon Czolgosz in Buffalo, New York; Theodore Roosevelt becomes president. Benjamin Harrison dies in Indianapolis, Indiana.

1902—U.S. acquires perpetual control over Panama Canal.

1903—Alaskan frontier is settled.

1904—Russian-Japanese War breaks out. Theodore Roosevelt wins presidential election.

1905—Treaty of Portsmouth signed, ending Russian-Japanese War.

1906—U.S. troops occupy Cuba.

1907—President Roosevelt bars all Japanese immigration. Oklahoma enters the Union.

1908—William Howard Taft becomes president. Grover Cleveland dies in Princeton, New Jersey. Lyndon B. Johnson is born near Stonewall, Texas.

1909—NAACP is founded under W.E.B. DuBois

1910—China abolishes slavery.

1911—Chinese Revolution begins. Ronald Reagan is born in Tampico, Illinois.

1912—Woodrow Wilson is elected president. Arizona and New Mexico become states.

1913—Federal income tax is introduced in U.S. through the Sixteenth Amendment. Richard Nixon is born in Yorba Linda, California. Gerald Ford is born in Omaha, Nebraska.

1914—World War I begins.

1915—British liner *Lusitania* is sunk by German submarine.

1916—Wilson is reelected president.

1917—U.S. breaks diplomatic relations with Germany. Czar Nicholas of Russia abdicates as revolution begins. U.S. declares war on Austria-Hungary. John F. Kennedy is born in Brookline, Massachusetts.

1918—Wilson proclaims "Fourteen Points" as war aims. On November 11, armistice is signed between Allies and Germany.

1919—Eighteenth Amendment prohibits sale and manufacture of intoxicating liquors. Wilson presides over first League of Nations; wins Nobel Peace Prize. Theodore Roosevelt dies in Oyster Bay, New York.

1920—Nineteenth Amendment (women's suffrage) is passed. Warren Harding is elected president.

1921—Adolf Hitler's stormtroopers begin to terrorize political opponents.

1922—Irish Free State is established. Soviet states form USSR. Benito Mussolini forms Fascist government in Italy.

1923—President Harding dies in San Francisco, California; he is succeeded by Vice-President Calvin Coolidge.

1924—Coolidge is elected president. Woodrow Wilson dies in Washington, D.C. James Carter is born in Plains, Georgia.

1925—Hitler reorganizes Nazi Party and publishes first volume of *Mein Kampf.*

1926—Fascist youth organizations founded in Germany and Italy. Republic of Lebanon proclaimed.

1927—Stalin becomes Soviet dictator. Economic conference in Geneva attended by fifty-two nations.

1928—Herbert Hoover is elected president. U.S. and many other nations sign Kellogg-Briand pacts to outlaw war.

1929—Stock prices in New York crash on "Black Thursday"; the Great Depression begins.

1930—Bank of U.S. and its many branches close (most significant bank failure of the year). William Howard Taft dies in Washington, D.C.

1931—Emigration from U.S. exceeds immigration for first time as Depression deepens.

1932—Franklin D. Roosevelt wins presidential election in a Democratic landslide.

1933—First concentration camps are erected in Germany. U.S. recognizes USSR and resumes trade. Twenty-First Amendment repeals prohibition. Calvin Coolidge dies in Northampton, Massachusetts.

1934—Severe dust storms hit Plains states. President Roosevelt passes U.S. Social Security Act.

1936—Roosevelt is reelected. Spanish Civil War begins. Hitler and Mussolini form Rome-Berlin Axis.

1937—Roosevelt signs Neutrality Act.

1938—Roosevelt sends appeal to Hitler and Mussolini to settle European problems amicably.

1939—Germany takes over Czechoslovakia and invades Poland, starting World War II.

1940—Roosevelt is reelected for a third term.

1941—Japan bombs Pearl Harbor. U.S. declares war on Japan. Germany and Italy declare war on U.S.; U.S. then declares war on them.

1942—Allies agree not to make separate peace treaties with the enemies. U.S. government transfers more than 100,000 Nisei (Japanese-Americans) from west coast to inland concentration camps.

1943—Allied bombings of Germany begin.

1944—Roosevelt is reelected for a fourth term. Allied forces invade Normandy on D-Day.

1945—President Franklin D. Roosevelt dies in Warm Springs, Georgia; Vice-President Harry S. Truman succeeds him. Mussolini is killed; Hitler commits suicide. Germany surrenders. U.S. drops atomic bomb on Hiroshima; Japan surrenders: end of World War II.

1946—U.N. General Assembly holds its first session in London. Peace conference of twenty-one nations is held in Paris.

1947—Peace treaties are signed in Paris. "Cold War" is in full swing.

1948—U.S. passes Marshall Plan Act, providing $17 billion in aid for Europe. U.S. recognizes new nation of Israel. India and Pakistan become free of British rule. Truman is elected president.

1949—Republic of Eire is proclaimed in Dublin. Russia blocks land route access from Western Germany to Berlin; airlift begins. U.S., France, and Britain agree to merge their zones of occupation in West Germany. Apartheid program begins in South Africa.

1950—Riots in Johannesburg, South Africa, against apartheid. North Korea invades South Korea. U.N. forces land in South Korea and recapture Seoul.

1951—Twenty-Second Amendment limits president to two terms.

1952—Dwight D. Eisenhower resigns as supreme commander in Europe and is elected president.

1953—Stalin dies; struggle for power in Russia follows. Rosenbergs are executed for espionage.

1954—U.S. and Japan sign mutual defense agreement.

1955—Blacks in Montgomery, Alabama, boycott segregated bus lines.

1956—Eisenhower is reelected president. Soviet troops march into Hungary.

1957—U.S. agrees to withdraw ground forces from Japan. Russia launches first satellite, *Sputnik*.

1958—European Common Market comes into being. Alaska becomes the forty-ninth state. Fidel Castro begins war against Batista government in Cuba.

1959—Hawaii becomes fiftieth state. Castro becomes premier of Cuba. De Gaulle is proclaimed president of the Fifth Republic of France.

1960—Historic debates between Senator John F. Kennedy and Vice-President Richard Nixon are televised. Kennedy is elected president. Brezhnev becomes president of USSR.

1961—Berlin Wall is constructed. Kennedy and Khrushchev confer in Vienna. In Bay of Pigs incident, Cubans trained by CIA attempt to overthrow Castro.

1962—U.S. military council is established in South Vietnam.

1963—Riots and beatings by police and whites mark civil rights demonstrations in Birmingham, Alabama; 30,000 troops are called out. Martin Luther King, Jr., is arrested. Freedom marchers descend on Washington, D.C., to demonstrate. President Kennedy is assassinated in Dallas, Texas; Vice-President Lyndon B. Johnson is sworn in as president.

1964—U.S. aircraft bomb North Vietnam. Johnson is elected president. Herbert Hoover dies in New York City.

1965—U.S. combat troops arrive in South Vietnam.

1966—Thousands protest U.S. policy in Vietnam. National Guard quells race riots in Chicago.

1967—Six-Day War between Israel and Arab nations.

1968—Martin Luther King, Jr., is assassinated in Memphis, Tennessee. Senator Robert Kennedy is assassinated in Los Angeles. Riots and police brutality take place at Democratic National Convention in Chicago. Richard Nixon is elected president. Czechoslovakia is invaded by Soviet troops.

1969—Dwight D. Eisenhower dies in Washington, D.C. Hundreds of thousands of people in several U.S. cities demonstrate against Vietnam War.

1970—Four Vietnam War protesters are killed by National Guardsmen at Kent State University in Ohio.

1971—Twenty-Sixth Amendment allows eighteen-year-olds to vote.

1972—Nixon visits Communist China; is reelected president in near-record landslide. Watergate affair begins when five men are arrested in the Watergate hotel complex in Washington, D.C. Nixon announces resignations of aides Haldeman, Ehrlichman, and Dean and Attorney General Kleindienst as a result of Watergate-related charges. Harry S. Truman dies in Kansas City, Missouri.

1973—Vice-President Spiro Agnew resigns; Gerald Ford is named vice-president. Vietnam peace treaty is formally approved after nineteen months of negotiations. Lyndon B. Johnson dies in San Antonio, Texas.

1974—As a result of Watergate cover-up, impeachment is considered; Nixon resigns and Ford becomes president. Ford pardons Nixon and grants limited amnesty to Vietnam War draft evaders and military deserters.

1975—U.S. civilians are evacuated from Saigon, South Vietnam, as Communist forces complete takeover of South Vietnam.

1976—U.S. celebrates its Bicentennial. James Earl Carter becomes president.

1977—Carter pardons most Vietnam draft evaders, numbering some 10,000.

1980—Ronald Reagan is elected president.

1981—President Reagan is shot in the chest in assassination attempt. Sandra Day O'Connor is appointed first woman justice of the Supreme Court.

1983—U.S. troops invade island of Grenada.

1984—Reagan is reelected president. Democratic candidate Walter Mondale's running mate, Geraldine Ferraro, is the first woman selected for vice-president by a major U.S. political party.

1985—Soviet Communist Party secretary Konstantin Chernenko dies; Mikhail Gorbachev succeeds him. U.S. and Soviet officials discuss arms control in Geneva. Reagan and Gorbachev hold summit conference in Geneva. Racial tensions accelerate in South Africa.

1986—Space shuttle *Challenger* explodes shortly after takeoff; crew of seven dies. U.S. bombs bases in Libya. Corazon Aquino defeats Ferdinand Marcos in Philippine presidential election.

1987—Iraqi missile rips the U.S. frigate *Stark* in the Persian Gulf, killing thirty-seven American sailors. Congress holds hearings to investigate sale of U.S. arms to Iran to finance Nicaraguan *contra* movement.

Index

Page numbers in boldface type indicate illustrations.

About the Author

Zachary Kent grew up in Little Falls, New Jersey, and received an English degree from St. Lawrence University. Following college he worked at a New York City literary agency for two years and then launched his writing career. To support himself while writing, he has worked as a taxi driver, a shipping clerk, and a house painter. Mr. Kent has had a lifelong interest in American history. Studying the U.S. presidents was his childhood hobby. His collection of presidential items includes books, pictures, and games, as well as several autographed letters.